To **Queen Kimberly**

From **Wanda**

Special Note

Oh what a Wonder you are!
Wonderfully & Fearfully Made
by God woman of God!!

Blessings
Love
Wanda

Book Completion Services Provided by:
TRU Statement
Publications | www.trustatementpublications.com

TRU Statement
PUBLICATIONS
www.trustatementpublications.com

First Edition: August 2021
Printed in the United States of America
0 8 1 4 2 0 2 1
ISBN: 978-1-948085-61-8

YOU ARE A QUEEN

BY WANDA MOORE

In Honor of Sharon Denise Torbert

A SPECIAL THANK YOU

I would like to thank my awesome and amazing husband for his continuous love and support. He has always allowed me to be me, and I am forever grateful. I really appreciate him from the bottom of my heart for staying strong and unwavering for our family. I will always admire and love him forever.

***

I want to say a big thank you to my sister, Dr. Misty Thomas, for never turning me away when I had an idea or even wanted her to proofread my content. Also, to thank her for taking time out of her busy schedule to meet up with me to go over the outline. Blessings, Dr. Thomas, to all your future endeavors!

***

To my Daughter, Queen Shambria, thank you for being so supportive of all of my endeavors. I would ask her what she thinks, and she will always be truthful. Thanks, Shambria, for being the loving and caring daughter that you are.

Love you forever, My Queen 👑

***

To My Supporters,

I want to thank you from the bottom of my heart. I pray that you are abundantly blessed, forever knowing that you are a Royalty.

***

CONTENTS

A TRIBUTE TO SHARON

What is a *Queen*? This is a question that I have asked myself several times throughout the years. And it is also one that comes with multiple different answers. My definition of a *Queen* is a woman who is not afraid to be herself. She is a woman who can say so little while still saying it all. She is a woman who remains strong regardless of any obstacles she may face. She is a woman who can light up the darkest of rooms. She is the same woman who can turn your worst day into the best day ever.

Although she may not be perfect, she knows that she is beautiful inside and out. Now, I ask myself who was this lovely lady?! This *Queen* was my mother, Sharon Denise Torbert. No words could ever express how much she is missed and loved. And even though she gained a halo, she will always carry a crown.

~ Keyonna Torbert

My mother was a Beautiful *Queen*! From the crown of her head to the souls of her feet. She dressed to *impress* every time she stepped out. The flawless lashes, bold earrings, & even the eye-catching shoes she wore described her to a T. The cards, gifts, and even the newspaper shout-outs were nothing short of amazing. So admired for her passion for others! Our Mother, forever in our hearts! Love you Always!

~ Sweet

Grandma Sharon was sweet and funny, just like me. I liked it when she spent the night with us, and she used to say, "Hush that fuss up," (lol). She was one of a kind. I loved when she used to let me spend the day with her. We used to have some much fun. I love you, grandma.

~ Taylor

 grandma was something serious! We had a good bond. She loved her jewelry and big earrings. Oh yeah, I can't forget her designer bags. The thing that she like to do was watch her lifetime. I could sit with her all day and watch lifetime with her.

When she beginning to get sick, we got closer. I began to see her every day and we would ride around and go eat. If it's one thing I learned from her, it was to always look presentable. As long as I could remember, I never seen her go anywhere without lookin' her best! Sharon Denise dressed to impress!

~ *Tyasia Williams*

Aunt, Sharon, was the flyest women I knew. She always had the best clothes, shoes, purses, and jewelry. As a child, I always thought that she was what it was like to be a woman. Her hair was always done, her nails were always freshly manicured, and her lashes were always on point. Even though I did live far away from my Aunt Sharon, if she did have a bad day, I never saw it or heard about it!

In watching the way she lived her life, she taught me to always be about my business and to never let no one see you sweat. Even if you are down on your luck, always hold your head high and be proud of whatever it is you are doing. If you said it, you said it. If you did it, you did it. Hold your head high and keep it moving, regardless of what anyone has to say about you. Be proud of who you are!

~ *Shalicia L. Torbert*

 Sharon, what can I say? She was a very unique individual who knew how to dress and kept up with the latest fashion trends. This is one person you had to know to love. This is the aunt who would let you get away with everything. I loved to go over to her house. At her house you could eat whatever. I remember when we were younger, she would buy us whatever we wanted.

As I grew older, we grew apart. We would still talk at times, but not as much as we had while I was still in school. That is what alerted me that something was going on with Aunt Sharon. Even though I could not figure out what was wrong initially, I would still try to make efforts to communicate with her to show her that I was still there for her. I was thankfully able to reconnect with her at our family reunion that was held a few months before her death. I am thankful for t' last conversations and talks that we had. J my aunt Sharon!

~ S

I am forever grateful for my 28-year relationship with my sister-in-law, Sharon Denise Torbert. There was no one else like her! The definition of 'Bling, Glitz & Glamour!' She was definitely 'The One & Only!' She was flamboyant, fierce and truly a free spirit, living her life unapologetically and without restraint! I know she loved her family very much. In her own way, she demonstrated that love often. She will forever be missed. OUR *Queen*, Sharon!

~ *Yvette Torbert*

My gifted/talented niece, Tyasia, hosted a paint party for my 49th birthday. This is when God gave me the title, You Are a Queen!

Looking at all the paintings, the Lord showed me that Sharon was already a Queen, but she didn't walk it out according to His plan.

Sharon was gone too soon.

***

You Are a Queen

DEDICATION TO MOM QUEEN ETTA

This dedication is to the strongest *Queen* I have ever known. I call her '*Queen* Etta,' my mom. Mom has come through many obstacles in life over these 80 years, and praise be to God, she is yet standing! She is the only survivor out of her 5 siblings!

I have watched my mother live by faith and trusting God through it all. I have never seen her 'break to stay broken.' Mom has endured the loss of two children: Ronnie and Sharon. In 2018, we lost dad and our sister, *Queen* Sharon, 6 weeks apart unexpectedly. Mom was heartbroken. Her inward strength, the power of God, and our family support helped her make it through.

God has been faithful and amazing to *Queen* Etta. We are sooo honored to call her the blessed *Queen* that God has placed His seal of approval upon in our city! She is indeed our strength. We love you, *Queen* Etta.

Queen Etta

You Are a Queen

PROLOGUE

You Are a Queen is inspired and dedicated to a strong woman who proves that it is not one's life journey that makes one a *Queen*, but the grace, elegance, and strength she exhibits during the journey. This amazing *Queen* is my late sister, Sharon Denise Torbert.

Two days before my forty-ninth birthday, Sharon's journey ended suddenly on September sixth, two thousand-eighteen. Sharon's passing was a devastating loss to me and our family. Although gone in present, she has remained in both my heart and memories.

Our family resided in the Mitchell quarter community in Beauregard, AL. Sharon was the eldest in our circle of siblings. My memories are filled with my childhood of Sharon, myself and our brothers, Ted and Tim. I still hear our joyous childlike laughs as we played and lived among the traditional country life at the hand of our father. I can still see him taking the chickens by the head, then ringing them by the neck until their heads fell off before placing the bodies in hot water to remove the feathers.

Beginning a promiscuous life at an early age, Sharon was welcomed into motherhood at the age of fifteen with the birth of her eldest daughter Tywanna. Sweet, we called Tywanna, as she became more of a sister than a niece to me after our parents raised her as their own.

It was years later, while I was in high school, when Sharon left home to live with her boyfriend. This began a pattern of Sharon returning, then leaving home. I am reminded of how she spent weekends away, then returning on Monday. This lifestyle resulted in her giving birth to three additional children by multiple fathers.

By looking at Sharon, one would have thought she had everything together. Sharon cared greatly about her appearance. She always dressed to impress and made sure to make her weekly appointments to both the nail and hair salon. This lifestyle gave off the impression she had a great job, but that was the furthest thing from the truth. Sharon had the mentality that she did not need to have a job to sustain herself. I can still hear her saying, "I don't need to work; my men take care of me." Sharon would constantly brag about how her men had a lot of money. Sharon always received what she wanted and would obtain these things by any means necessary.

My sister was never ashamed of her actions. Instead, she took pride in them. Starting at an early age, Sharon would use alias names to get credit cards. This included using my name, her children's names, and our mother's. I learned I could not trust my sister with anything, even my personal belongings.

As time passed, Sharon began telling lies, even to simple questions. A conversation with her consisted of sifting through her words of truth and lies. This new change opened my eyes to see her issues. I saw how she searched for love in all the wrong and dark places. The way she let men use her revealed she was naïve. It was heartbreaking to watch, as she would allow men to use her. Sharon gained fulfillment in the temporary recognition and attention she received from men.

No longer blinded to her flaws, my mind traced

back to her childhood, our childhood. Growing up, it became obvious that I was daddy's heart. From him calling me *babygirl* and always making a difference between Sharon and I, it was clear that daddy never recognized who she was.

Sharon was always the one to get in trouble first. I remember the time Sharon hit me so hard with a telephone that it caused a painful gash above my eye. When daddy came home and saw my injury, he gave Sharon a whooping like she'd never had before. I believe because of this difference my father made between Sharon and me, along with his mistreatment towards her, was the root of my sister's adult behavior and poor choices she made when it came to love. The lack of love she felt from her father sent her on a journey to find the love she never had.

As life continued this way for my sister, her behavior began to reflect the choices of her life. I witnessed my sister's life continue on this downward spiral, and many of us labeled her as the "crazy one," oblivious to her deep-rooted pain. Her behaviors began to amplify as she aged.

Sharon also began lashing out at me, and I can only assume this was caused by the envy she harbored for me because of our daddy's actions in the past. Sharon even started spreading lies about me to anyone who would listen. She made hurtful allegations that I wanted the men she was with at the time. This attack on my character even developed into her scandalizing my children's names, her own niece and nephew.

Although these things would hurt me, I could never bring myself to retaliate against her; instead, I charged this to her declining mental health. I knew my sister was sick. I also knew that those who knew my true character would not believe her lies. In the last few years of Sharon's life, it was hard witnessing her go through so many detrimental changes in her life. It began with her no longer taking pride in her appearance. She neglected both the nail and hair salon. She went on to become very paranoid, believing someone was out to get her. This led to her entering into a deep depression, yet she refused help.

Realizing there could be a benefit from her

illness, she finally sought out help for her mental state. She told our mom that a friend relayed to her that she could receive monetary benefits for her sickness. It was this decision that would cause her final downfall. Sharon was unaware of the strength in the medication the doctors prescribed to her. Unfortunately, she was also unaware of the side effects she would endure from not slowing weaning herself off of them, and instead she stopped taking her medication abruptly.

While attending several of Sharon's doctor appointments, I witnessed her not disclosing that she needed further help. I inquired about Sharon being placed in a mental facility as her health continued to decline, but her therapist informed me that Sharon could not be placed into a mental facility without her willful consent.

It was the last week of Sharon's life when she told me she would seek help. Her only request was if she could check herself into a facility outside of our city. The day before her journey ended, I can recall our last conversation. I was at an eye appointment when she called and asked if I would call her eldest son and ask him to bring her a large, sweet tea from McDonalds. I told her I would and did.

Calling her once again after my eye appointment, I assured her if her son did not come to bring the sweet tea, I or her oldest daughter would. That was the last time I spoke to my sister. Sharon was truly sick, which resulted in her passing on September sixth.

In spite of everything that my sister went through, she still gave us loving moments we will never forget! My mind often goes back to her love of cooking and how much she loved to decorate her home. Every holiday you could hear the click-cling, sounding of brass of those pots and pans, ready to be heated and seasoned to her preferred taste. She would always cook my son his own personal pan of dressing. Not only did she cater to my son with a personal pan of dressing, but I am feeling sick thinking about those stinking hog chitterlings that she loved to cook and send to my husband as well. Despite my disdain for the awful smell in my house, I allowed my husband to bring them home, because he loved them so much!

Sharon took pride and had a deep love for her home, interior wall pictures, and her artificial standing trees. I have a picture that I glance at from time to time and will forever cherish the glimpses of my beloved sister that they give me. She will be forever missed by all her qualities she possessed. I can truly say that in the last few years of Sharon's life, she had changed and had a humbling spirit. I believe she realized that she needed her family more than she thought. Once she saw that I had forgiven and accepted her for all she had done, she felt comfortable enough to call me anytime.

In the midst of not knowing she would soon be gone, I made sure that I did whatever was necessary to help her get what she needed. I am thankful and grateful to God that I had forgiven my sister, unknowing that she would be gone from us so soon. The only regret I have today is that I could not get my sister the help she needed in time. Sharon is gone forever.

Sharon Denise Torbert

April 29, 1964-September 6, 2018

GOD'S PLAN
FOR A QUEEN

Jeremiah 29:11, "I know the thoughts and plans that I have for you, says the Lord, thoughts and plans for welfare and peace and not for evil, to give you hope in your final outcome."

God told Jeremiah, "I knew you in the womb." What one can take from this scripture is that God is giving one hope and comfort. He promises that He has a plan for our lives, regardless of the current situation we are in. Through God, one shall prosper. He knows who we are, what we are made to be, and what we can bear. We see this through God keeping His promise to Jeremiah and guiding him back to the original place He set before him.

The plan God has for a *Queen* will require consulting God on our thoughts and decisions. A *Queen* is to seek God's face and have faith in Him, no matter their current situation. A *Queen* knows it is not what it appears to be, but what it will be. God has ordered the *Queen's* steps and placed the whole armor of God on the *Queen* as her shield. A *Queen* must travel through her journey knowing that she is a *Queen* supplied with the power, guidance, and wisdom of God. Each step the *Queen* takes on her journey gets her closer to the end, where God has destined her to be.

It is essential to know oneself in God. This

knowledge is crucial because one must have a relationship with God to be able to discern His voice. There must be faith in God. These few things are a must because once a *Queen* has this knowledge and understanding, she can follow the plan that is set before her. Many potential *Queens* have left this earth, having never discovered their purpose and plan for life. My sister Sharon was one of those women. You are learning now how to have the power to prevent this from happening to yourself.

The *Queen* is in you, you already possess this status. Become her and walk in this role by asking the Lord to help you discover this wonderful gift. It is easy to see ourselves as one thing and let this false self-image keep one from discovering the *Queen* that God had designed them to be. This can block the fulfillment that God has planned for our lives.

Celebrating my forty-ninth birthday, I did so with a painting party. The image we were to paint was that of a *Queen*. When my sister Sharon missed my party, it was then that God gave me a revelation about Sharon. Sharon was a *Queen* but had no knowledge of this and would never discover this before passing. Sharon had it in her, she only needed to believe it for herself.

Learning from the experience of living life and traveling through my journey, I have discovered that there is plenty of time wasted in one's youth chasing after the null and void. As one lives on, getting older as each year passes, the realization of wasted time comes to mind, making room for regret. Indeed, this time cannot be bought back or tangibly retrieved. However, the *Queen* knows that it is never too late for change. Each day God blesses us with is a new day to begin again and make a change, leaving yesterday in the past. Moving forward is the key to discovering your identity.

As a *Queen*, it is imperative to make conscious decisions and to do things God's way. This is not just to please God, but to be able to walk, talk, and reign as a true *Queen*. I think back to the many days I prayed to God with a heart of hope and a mouth of request that He would turn Sharon around before it was too late. It is because of Sharon that I know all women are *Queens* and can discover this to reign as one. The *Queen* exists inside her from the time she is born. Being given a name is her being given her crown of royalty and title. This is where her journey begins, and this is when God places her on the path she will travel and triumph through.

Queen Status

Directions: Rate 0 to 5 how much you believe each statement. "0" means you do not believe it at all and "5" means you completely believe it. Take this quiz again at the completion of this book.

	STATEMENT	RATING
1.	I believe in myself.	_____
2.	I know who I am.	_____
3.	I am happy to be me.	_____
4.	I like the way I look.	_____
5.	I am just as valuable as others.	_____
6.	I see my past as a learning experience, not a failure.	_____
7.	I am a leader.	_____
8.	I can handle criticism.	_____
9.	I am proud of my accomplishments.	_____
10.	I respect myself.	_____
11.	I feel good when I receive compliments.	_____
12.	I am not afraid of making mistakes.	_____
13.	I would rather be me than someone else.	_____
14.	I know my worth.	_____
15.	I feel like a *Queen*.	_____
16.	I love myself even when I am rejected by others.	_____
17.	I ask for help when I need it.	_____
18.	I do not worry about what others think of me.	_____

TOTAL SCORE: _____

0-30 points	Becoming a *Queen*.
31-60 points	A *Queen* in the Making
61-90 points	Walking as a *Queen*.

WHO ARE YOU

At different stages of one's life, one is asked the traditional question, "Who Are You?" As a little girl, she may answer, "I'm a big girl." When this little girl becomes a child, she may answer "I'm mommy's or daddy's girl." Then the day will come between the age of her preteens and teenage years when she is asked, "Who are you?" and her mother, grandmother, mentor, or the woman in her life she admires will have to give her the answer to this question. This wise woman will tell this young lady that she is a *Queen* and open her blinded eyes to a new world.

Who are you? is and has become a challenging question to answer for all ages and stages of a woman's life. This is because it takes one's life experiences and what is put in her that will determine if she can answer this question. It is also determined by what stage of life she is currently in. Age will not determine if a lady can answer who she is. A lady can answer this through experience, the confidence that was placed in her. She can answer this by the examples she has seen around her, even her environment can aid in this answer.

A young woman stating who she is, is based on the experience she has had in the short time she has spent on earth. Some young ladies may have had a hard start, therefore now their confidence is low, and they are unsure of themselves. The other young lady who had a more pleasant upbringing will have more confidence. This can be because she has not experienced true struggle and only good things have been put into her. No matter the beginning, it will not dictate her outcome. The young lady who grows up with struggles of inconsistent healthy meals will grow up to be resourceful and take an interest in where food comes from. The young lady who had plenty grows up to be a *Queen* with a grateful and giving heart.

The mid to older woman will state who she is based on her past life experiences too. Her answers may have varied. She may begin confident at the beginning of life, however in the middle of life that confidence may lower, and her answer may vary. As more time goes on and she becomes wiser and learns the game of life, she is officially able to not only know who she is but explain why she is this person.

Life has a way of teaching lessons and teaching those lessons in creative and challenging ways. What appears like a failure should be a learning experience. What appears to be a challenge should be a defeatable obstacle. A realization that a mile is broken down to one step at a time. The hole in the ground is capable of being climbed out of. Knowing that one wounded arm does not take away the mobility of the other.

Becoming a *Queen*, she will know that all these things should not be regretted, but are necessary in molding her to be who she is meant to be. When asked, "Who are you?" she will now be able to say that she is a patient woman who never gives up. That her feet have traveled far, therefore her endurance is unstoppable. She knows what it is like to view a high goal from below, therefore being that she is here now is proof that one day you can look it eye-to-eye and achieve it. The mid to older woman is seasoned and life has helped in this development.

The goal answer to *Who are you?* is simply a *Queen*. This answer embodies everything a woman should be. From confident, intelligent, strong, beautiful, a supporter, a leader, a problem-solver and so many more characteristics that continue to elevate the woman. The uniqueness of a *Queen* is that she is an honored woman that others do not envy, but aspire to be her. The *Queen* acts as a young woman's example, and a person they aspire to become.

A *Queen* is an attitude. An attitude that is pleasant and makes her favorable among all. Her mindset and mood are not swayed by other reactions, attitudes, or behavior. A true *Queen* will never have an arrogant attitude because this is a sign of insecurity. The *Queen* is aware that everyone has value; all are worthy of being treated with kindness, respect, and love. The *Queen* is very aware of who she is and does not have to yell it out verbally, but it is said with her attitude and character.

This book should be used as a tool to become a *Queen* or to finish developing the *Queen* that already exists in you. Use this book as a steppingstone on your journey in life and pulling out the *Queen* inside you.

Being a *Queen* is obtainable because she is a known figure across the world and lives inside every woman. Every woman embodies a great and wise *Queen*. Being a *Queen* is not just a role given by birthright. Yes, there are born *Queens*, then there are made *Queens*. Both born and made *Queen* are valuable.

Right now, you are a young lady being molded into a *Queen*. By the end of this book, you, the reader, be it a young girl or woman, will say with full confidence, "I am a *Queen*." She will place the crown on her head, lifting her chin high with her head held up, and place a royal cloak around herself to show herself and the world, her royal stature. She will not only believe she is a *Queen* but know what this name and role means.

***

Description Of A Queen

A *Queen* is a worldwide known figure and one who has existed in some form since the beginning of time. Today her title may have changed, but she still holds the responsibility. For example, the wife of the president is called the First Lady. The First Lady is honored like a *Queen* and has her agenda from her husband to help improve the lives of others in some way.

Another *Queen* that is seen closer to home depending on religion is the wife of a church Preacher or Pastor. She is also known as First Lady and honored as a *Queen*. She serves and gives back to the congregation, all the while still holding her position as a leader.

As stated before, there are born *Queens* and made *Queens*. Beginning with the born *Queen*, this is a role that was destined for her through birthright. They began as a princess and became a *Queen*. They are taught the history of other *Queens* before them, a *Queen's* behavior, and are treated like a *Queen* before the title is officially placed on them in preparation for her future. Examples of this type of *Queen* have existed in different cultures and tribes. Some commonly known in history are Queen Nefertiti, Queen Cleopatra, Queen Elizabeth, etc.

Queens are made just as special, needed, and strong. These *Queens* are powerful, for they were made from experiences, life experiences. Made *Queens* can be prepared to a made leaders. This leader must have certain experiences to lead. Both, the made *Queen* and made leader, must learn and learn from others. *Others* can be a great way to learn because one can see what is successful in a situation. By observing others, this made *Queen* will see failures and learn problem-solving from these examples.

There are different ways of learning, being thrown into the water hoping to instantly learn how to swim to survive, learn from failures, or learn from sitting at the feet of the wise hearing cherished advice. A made *Queen* cannot be easily knocked down or tricked. They think quick on their feet. Life taught them this as well as tools and examples given to them. Examples of made

Queens are those who marry into a royal family, such as Marie Antoinette and *Queen* Charlotte.

Naturally, a *Queen* is known as regal, self-assured, well-spoken, wise, and has a reputation that she is proud of. *Queens* are desired because of the way they carry themselves and how this behavior is not just portrayed in front of others openly, but even in private she still is and behaves like a *Queen*.

Power also comes with being a *Queen*, however, she knows how to use this at the appropriate times and keeps it in balance. It is a great skill; she must be able to have power and remain humble and to know what is best for herself, even if it will be a challenging experience. For example, having to make temporary sacrifices to reach the ending goal.

A Queen is you!

***

Qualities Of A Queen

The qualities of a *Queen* can be seen instantly, easily, and be remembered. *Queens* have charisma, confidence, giving back, speech, great attire, and have a great attitude. Learning all these traits and mastering them will not only pull out the *Queen* that exists inside of you, but will develop her and become your identity.

Charisma. The definition of charisma is compelling attractiveness or charm that can inspire devotion in others. This means she is likable and has good and high energy. This *Queen* keeps a bright and genuine smile on her face that she freely gives to all. She is very friendly and not afraid to greet others. She attracts many with her charisma. Her charisma makes up a lot of her personality and is her first impression to the world.

Confidence. The definition of confidence is a feeling of self-assurance arising from one's appreciation of one's abilities or qualities. Confidence exudes in a *Queen* without her having to announce it or bring attention to her confidence. Imagine the woman that walks into a room and grabs the attention of both men and women. She does not have to be the best dressed or say a word. It is all in how she walks in with her head held high and her posture, her shoulders back, giving her a taller look. This is the quality you must have as a *Queen*. Confidence is key because it is the glue to all the qualities of a *Queen*. It is the full package and is a part of her outward and inner beauty.

Giving back. To give back means to provide help to others without wanting anything in return or wanting recognition. When a *Queen* has something to give, she does willingly. Some examples are donating her time through volunteering such as tutoring students, serving food, or cooking food in a shelter, and picking up trash in a park or on the side of the road. A *Queen* is not selfish and thinks of others as well as herself. Giving back comes from the *Queen's* heart. It is like second nature to her. A *Queen* knows to have a strong community, she must give back to it. She knows the action of giving back is powerful, verses only discussing the issues.

Speech. The definition of speech is the expression of or the ability to express thoughts and feelings. A *Queen* speaks eloquently and clearly and is understood by many. The *Queen* knows when to listen, then when to speak. The skill of listening strengths her ability to speak. She annunciates her words and has a great vocabulary. Her tone is calm and not overpowering. She never uses profanity or yells. This skill takes practice and studying. An easy way to master these skills is to read and read many different types of books. Speech is important not only to be understood but to be able to speak openly; and when called on, she is able to speak confidently, even when unprepared.

Great Attire. To have great attire, one does not have to spend hundreds or even thousands on an outfit. The key is to look neat, give a taste of your personality, and dress tastefully leaving parts of your body to the imagination. Having a few great quality staple pieces can go a long way and be layered. For example, having a black blazer, white-collared shirt, black jeans, blue jeans, a jacket, and a nice coat.

The next key is to accessorize. Add pops of colors with earrings or if wearing a simple black dress, wear a statement necklace. In all, a *Queen* dresses neatly for her size, tasteful, and with a pop of her personality.

A *Queen* keeps in mind that she can be fashionable all while dressing in feminine, modest, and timeless wear. There is a time and place for pajamas, sweatpants, and satin caps/bonnets. A *Queen* is mindful of which attire is appropriate for what occasion. She keeps in mind the dress code for events and places she attends.

Attitude. An attitude is a combination of how one behaves towards others and treats others. A *Queen* has a winning attitude. She does not take her frustrations out on others. Sometimes one may not be able to help how they feel, however one can control their reaction and behavior — a *Queen* knows this.

The other great side of attitude is it can be used to drive you towards goals. Such as making the *Queen* ambitious, being proactive, and seeking opportunities. Her attitude can affect her outcome in life. The *Queen* is aware that she will go further with a positive attitude versus having a negative attitude.

POSITIVE
EXPERIENCE
KEEPSAKES

Directions: On the following pages, briefly write about times when you displayed each of the following qualities.

Positive Experience Keepsakes

COURAGE

Positive Experience Keepsakes

KINDNESS

Positive Experience Keepsakes

LOVE

Positive Experience Keepsakes

SACRIFICE

Positive Experience Keepsakes

CONFIDENCE

Positive Experience Keepsakes

DETERMINATION

You Are a Queen

EXAMPLES OF A
QUEEN

Queen Esther was chosen to be the *Queen* among one hundred women. Esther was unbelievably beautiful, and her beauty exceeded her. Esther was known for her beauty before anything else.

Esther was a Jew, an orphan raised by her cousin Mordecai. King Xerxes hosted a royal beauty pageant to find his new *Queen*. During the preparations of the women who also were chosen to participate in this royal pageant, Esther was a woman who found favor among all the king's staff and palace and was chosen to be the *Queen*. Esther was the most famous of the *Queens*. She is also the only *Queen* that has a book of the Bible named after her. Esther is also widely known for her actions when she reigned as a *Queen*.

During this time, King Xerxes' highest official, Haman, hated Jews and wanted them to bow down to him. When Esther's cousin Mordecai refused, Haman devised a scheme that the king approved to have all Jews killed. When Esther learned from this from her cousin Mordecai, Esther fasted and prayed before going before the king, which was a risk for her life on behalf of her people. Esther had a wish that her life and her people be spared. Esther was the one who stood in the gap for her people. For her strength, faith, and confidence, her life, and her people were spared, and Haman was killed.

Esther teaches us that at times, to be a *Queen* requires a woman to take risks and follow her instinct and to never sway from her morals and values. Becoming a *Queen* did not cause Esther to forget who she was and where she came from. This is important to remember as a *Queen* Esther's past and upbringing taught her to fast, pray, and have faith, a tool she used in her fight.

As a *Queen*, you may never know what you will have to use from your past to fight. Esther also shows us that she was the full package and ready to be a *Queen*. She had a *Queen's* beauty, a *Queen's* wisdom and knowledge. Esther had a *Queen's* attitude and courage. Esther was also led by wise counsel, Mordecai. Esther is also a wonderful example of how a great *Queen* will sacrifice. She sacrificed her life for her people and beliefs. One can learn from Esther that there is more to beauty. The *Queen* must be the full package and not afraid to put herself out in the world or in any situation which she is confident that she can overcome.

THE QUEEN IN ME

Things I am Good At:	Compliments I Have Received:
1.	1.
2.	2.
3.	3.
What I like About My Appearance:	**Challenges I Have Overcome:**
1.	1.
2.	2.
3.	3.

I Have Helped Others By:	Things That Make Me Unique:
1.	1.
2.	2.
3.	3.
What I Value Most:	**Times I Have Made Others Happy:**
1.	1.
2.	2.
3.	3.

Queen Checklist

○ A *Queen* knows who she is.

○ You can learn to be a *Queen* from another *Queen*, Mother, Grandmother, Guardian, or Mentor.

○ There are *Queens* that are born *Queens* and *Queens* that are made *Queens*.

○ First Ladies are today's *Queens*.

○ *Queens* have charisma, confidence, give back, speak well, dress well, and have a great attitude.

○ Ester is a great example of a *Queen*.

○ *Queens* learn from their past and by observing others.

○ A *Queen* is already inside you.

○ *Queens* hold their held up high, with their shoulders back.

○ *Queens* never sway from their morals and values to accommodate trends.

○ A *Queen* is a leader.

○ *Queens* are humble but powerful.

○ A *Queen's* behavior tells others she is a *Queen*.

○ *Queens* have reputations they are proud of.

○ *Queens* are examples to others.

○ It takes time and practice to become a *Queen*.

○ Knowing who you are is just as important as behaving as a *Queen*.

○ Being a *Queen* is an honor.

***

QUEEN AFFIRMATION

I Can and I Will.

I Am Enough!

You Are a Queen

KNOW YOUR
WORTH

Knowing ones worth will usually come with the passing of time and numerous lessons learned. Commonly in the end it may be stated learning one's worth. In the case of a *Queen*, she must know her worth from the day the title is placed on her. Looking back in history, a *Queen* walked in her status, knew her worth; all she was told was that she was a *Queen*.

A true *Queen* knows her worth, and she does not ask for it. The *Queen* states it with her regal attitude, walk, leadership, and having a heart for others. A *Queen* never accepts anything less than her worth. Some examples of knowing one's worth are not settling for just any kind of love just to have love in one's life and not accepting one to speak to you in a rude manner or tone.

A *Queen* knows how to respectfully demand respect from others. When the best is available, she accepts it, knowing it is what she deserves. Knowing your worth is not allowing others to bring you down. The *Queen* knows she is worth knowing, loving, and finding. She has a mind of her own and it is moved by the opinions of herself, not others. This knowing your worth is having an awareness of who you are and your value. When a *Queen* inhabits this trait of knowing her worth, it comes off as an attractive quality. She appears confident in the world and draws others to her.

The *Queen* is beautiful both inside and out. It is important to love yourself first, above all things, to achieve this high self-worth. Having this quality does not let fear of life's challenges stop her from trekking forward. See, the beauty resides in yourself and not what others define as beauty.

A simple way to know your worth is to begin by knowing your rights as a *Queen*. The rights of a *Queen* are simple to understand, state, and live by. She knows these rights and navigates through life living by them. A *Queen* understands that rights are not privileges and not just for some, but for all. These are the following rights: A *Queen* has the right to...

Say No. A powerful, yet simple word that must be in any woman's vocabulary, especially a *Queen*, is "No." Saying 'No' is a right and depending on how one uses this word, as well as how often one uses it, tells of this woman's worth. Being able to use the word 'No' is a great quality that a *Queen* possesses. A *Queen* will use the word 'No' if she feels a situation or opportunity may not be a good fit for her. For example, one could be asked to lead a committee or group in a project. If the *Queen* feels or knows this project will require more time and commitment than she can currently sacrifice, saying 'No' is an appropriate answer, verses a 'Yes.'

The *Queen* knows that saying 'No' in this situation does not mean that she is incapable of leading. She knows it is better to give your best and all to a project verses taking on a task that could overwhelm her and bring about stress.

Another way a *Queen* will use the word 'No' may be standing firm on her beliefs and values. If she is asked to do something or participate in anything that goes against her beliefs and values, the *Queen* will answer "No" to this request verses answering "Yes," therefore turning against what she lives by. Recognizing saying 'No' as a right is a *Queen* trait because it is easy to answer 'Yes' to avoid confrontation, appease others, appear easy going, or easy to get along with, and lastly, to not stand out. Voicing 'No' means you know your worth because you know what you are or are not willing to do, you know your value, and you realize that pleasing others at the sacrifice of your happiness and peace of mind is no way to live as a mentally healthy *Queen*.

Express How You Feel. A *Queen* knows that there are times she has the right to say and show how she feels. Expressing the way one feels is natural. Expression of feelings comes in the form of laughing, crying, screaming, or using facial expressions, body language and the use of words. For example, instead of hiding sadness with a plastered smile, a *Queen* knows she can cry to express her feelings of sadness. There is strength in tears as it shows truth and empathy. Tears also portray that the *Queen* is also relatable and human.

A *Queen* can use her words to express her feelings both honestly and affectively without losing her grace, positive temperament, and power. Telling someone that they have upset you is just as much as a right as telling someone they brightened your day. Telling others how you feel allows others to know that you respect yourself. It says that you are willing to be honest with feelings that are negative and positive, verses only expressing the positive while hiding the negative.

Change Your Mind. A *Queen* can change her mind and feel no guilt for doing so. One must make numerous decision a day, some simple and some complex. One also must make life decisions that not only will have a greater effect on that person's life, but also the outcome. With this said, the changing of the mind can occur.

Many times, a person will remain in an unpleasant or miserable position or place by not wanting to change their mind, because this seems unacceptable. However, changing one's mind is a right. Changing one mind about the color of paint chosen for an accent wall in a home is acceptable, just as one wanting to change their mind about a career.

For some, this may look like changing your major in college or deciding you want to work for yourself as opposed to someone else. A *Queen* knows that changing your mind can be healthy when done in reason, because it can cause you to have to try something new.

Make Mistakes. Another way to think about the word 'mistake,' is to refer it to a life lesson. In life, there is a need for mistakes. Making mistakes is a great tool in life to learn and grow as a person. Taking a wrong turn while traveling teaches one about navigation and how to manage frustration to problem-solve. Being critiqued on a task, where you have made a mistake, will help you learn for the next opportunity and fewer mistakes will be made.

A *Queen* knows that she does not always have to complete tasks without mistakes, she only must give her best and it is about the execution. A *Queen* will make mistakes. What sets her apart from others is her ability to learn from them. Her ability to keep walking forward in life with her head held high, not looking back at her mistakes.

Over time, the *Queen* will make less mistakes because she will have both knowledge and wisdom to navigate through life. Know that as a *Queen*, it is necessary to make mistakes because it is a hands-on learning experience, and you have that right.

Be Imperfect. Wanting to achieve a title of being perfect is unrealistic and places a stressful type of pressure on one's shoulder. Many will spend great energy trying to be perfect as well as trying to please others. As a *Queen,* she knows that there is beauty in the imperfections of herself and others.

Being imperfect gives every one of us our personality. Being imperfect can be translated to many different things. Not being able to dance at society's standard of perfect dancing may seem like a reason to never dance or only dance in private. However, the imperfect dancer dances with joy, carefree, and from the heart.

Perfect is an idea, not a realistic and tangible thing. Embrace your imperfections as a *Queen*. Use it to encourage others that to be a leader or a *Queen*, one does not have to be perfect, but has the attitude and heart of a leader and *Queen*.

Ask for Help. Asking for help can be a challenge for many; however, the *Queen* uses this to her advantage and knows this is a tool. A *Queen* asks for help in two ways: learning a new skill and by delegation.

A *Queen* leads and mentors and for her team or mentee to learn from her, she knows they must ask questions to understand. The *Queen* at one point was under the leadership of another and had to ask for help or ask questions to improve her skills and master new information.

A *Queen* asks for help is by delegating. To delegate is to entrust someone with a task or responsibility. This is a form of help for another. This helps with spreading out large amounts of responsibility. Asking for help in this way is not a sign of weakness, but instead a sign of strength. A

Queen knows that she cannot do it all, therefore, asking for help will get the job done efficiently, timely, and stress free. There is wisdom in asking for help and bridges a *Queen* with others.

Make Your Own Choices. What sets a *Queen* apart from others is the fact that she makes her own decisions and choices. There are many influences today and a *Queen* knows how to make her own choices despite the influence. It is also important to keep in mind that as a *Queen* you do not have to apologize for your choices either. A *Queen* is guided by her intuition and praying for guidance. A *Queen* thinks for herself and keeps in mind the well-being of others.

***

Tips For a Queen
To Find Her Self-Worth

1. Do Not Compare Yourself to Others.

A *Queen* knows that she is her own person and is made uniquely by God. Nothing about her is a mistake. Society and the presence of social media have made it easy to compare ourselves to others. It influences how we feel we should look, speak, the things we should like, how we dress, and even the foods we eat. It is important to know that what may work for one person may not work for another.

Living a life of constant comparison will bring about negative thoughts and feelings towards yourself and take away from your confidence. A *Queen* knows how to admire others, all the while still seeing the beauty in herself no matter what size she is, the color of her skin, or the texture of her hair. If necessary, take a break from social media to find your worth.

2. Do What Makes You Feel Good.

Today we live in a time where society freely gives their opinion on women. There are opinions about what size women should be, women should wear less make-up, have long straightened hair, work certain jobs, be able to cook, and the endless list goes on.

To be a *Queen*, you must keep in mind that God has given us one life to live, only one. Take advantage of that and do what makes you feel good and overall happy. Life will be miserable living by the opinions of others. If you want short hair, cut it. If you want to be a firefighter, go for it. This life is yours and yours only. Live doing what YOU as a *Queen* wants to do.

3. Define Yourself.

Being a *Queen* is knowing who you are. A way to discover yourself is to try new things or experiences. To travel, try different hobbies until you find the one you love. Explore your interests. Keep in mind that there is no wrong or right way to be you; just embrace who you are and love that woman. Be yourself and the world will embrace you and know who you are. Being your authentic self will say so much about you and will open you up to a broader world.

4. Invest in Yourself.

As a *Queen,* it is vital to invest in yourself. Investing in yourself will make you the *Queen* you want to be. To be a wise and intelligent *Queen*, invest in your education. Focus on mastering what you learn in school. Read to continue to educate yourself. Consider furthering your education through college. Learn a trade or earn a certification. Always be willing to learn.

A *Queen* invests in her health. Investing in her health does not have to be driven by losing weight or trying to achieve a certain look. It is important to be in good health to be able to do the works of a *Queen*. Simple ways to be healthy is to drink water, have a balanced diet, and be active: walking, dancing, yoga, sports, etc.

Invest in your appearance. Keep in mind quality over quantity. Having good quality clothing gives a clean, chic, and polished look. Investing in your appearance also includes basic grooming. This includes regular visits to the dentist, taking care of your hair, keeping neat and clean nails, and adding optional additional touches, such as wearing make-up, perfume, and jewelry.

Lastly, invest in self-care. It is important for a *Queen* to take time for herself. Take a day off to pamper yourself, have a spa day, or get a massage. Invest in a nice vacation or treat yourself to a nice meal at a restaurant instead of cooking. In all, you are important, and investing in yourself is just as important as investing in others.

5. Stand Up for Yourself.

A *Queen* makes things happen and sometimes to do this, she must stand her ground and stand up for herself. Being a *Queen* does not exempt you from being challenged by others or life, however this does not mean you have to back down or wait for someone else to come to your rescue. When the time is appropriate, it is acceptable to defend yourself in a decision you make that may not be favorable to others.

A *Queen* can stand on up for her beliefs and not waiver based on other thoughts or opinions. If a *Queen* does not stand up for herself, she may be overlooked, walked over, not respected, or must wait a long time for another to defend her.

Things That Make Me Beautiful

*On the following lines, write character traits you
have and reasons you are beautiful.*

Queen Affirmations

*I Look Good. I Feel Good. I Am Good.
And There Is No One Else Like Me.*

***

I Love Being Me.

***

*I Believe in Myself and Abilities. I Am
Perfect Just the Way I Am.*

***

*I Am Worthy of Happiness, Love, Health,
Peace And Success.*

You Are a Queen

BUILDING MY QUEENDOM

Now that we have learned who a *Queen* is and her character traits, it is time to build yourself up as a *Queen* and create the Queendom or life you will reign in. A Queendom is where a *Queen* reigns, for you your Queendom is your life.

Your surroundings, and those that you keep around you, really do sum up who you are. It is important to be mindful of the company you keep and the things you keep around you. A key to a healthy mentality is to have a peaceful home and surround yourself with positive and motivated people. A Queendom has many elements, and a *Queen* keeps a healthy and thriving Queendom through balance and positivity.

Building your Queendom begins with the resources you have as a *Queen*. Resources help one to function effectively. Resources are like tools and are a part of staying organized. When life gets stressful, a *Queen* will pull from her toolbox of resources to help both guide her and get her through.

The main location of your Queendom is in your mind, therefore mental health is especially important and something that a *Queen* knows to monitor. The mind is immensely powerful and can affect your mood, outlook and what you prioritize. The following are some helpful resources that a *Queen* should possess.

***

Queen Affirmations

I Release All Past Trauma and Pain.

I Replace It With Love and Forgiveness.

Mental Health Resources

Celebrate the Good. It is crucial as a *Queen* to celebrate the good and good moments. Doing this creates great memories that will remain with a *Queen* through her journey. Celebrating the good replaces the opportunity to focus on the negatives of life. Good outweighs all. Take the time to celebrate it so that it can last.

Call a Friend. Keep good company, and more importantly, loyal and positive friends or a friend around you can be helpful in many ways. The resource of calling a friend can be used as a social call for enjoyment, great and uplifting conversation and to reminisce on past times.

Another way to use this resource is to call a friend for advice, comfort, to help motivate, and to be a non-judgmental ear to vent to. Having a loyal, positive, and trustworthy friend to be able to call on is an essential resource in a Queendom.

Slow Down. As a *Queen*, always remember to slow down and take time to smell the roses. Rushing through life will cause you to miss out on many beautiful, small moments. Take a moment to look at the night's sky and admire the stars. Take in the sweet sound of nature and simply slow down. Slowing down will help bring balance to a hectic and busy life and help to step back from stressful situations.

Read the Bible. If you are looking for guidance and understanding, the bible is a great tool and resource to have. There is much wisdom in the bible and exceptional stories filled with lessons and examples to help one in life. The bible connects us to God.

A *Queen* needs guidance and leadership, and the bible will give this to her. Having a religious core gives one value and morals to live by and a foundation to build upon. As a *Queen* you will learn many of your questions can be answered through reading the bible.

Trash Negative Thoughts. Negative thoughts are just that, thoughts. However, negative thoughts and be detrimental to the mind of a *Queen*. Negativity in the mind can stop progress, slow down motivation, and keep you from amazing opportunities and adventures. To keep a healthy mind, a *Queen* must instantly trash negative thoughts. When the thought arises, "I failed at that task," instead think, "That didn't work, but maybe this will."

Trashing negative thoughts is key to being a strong leader and keeping the traits and confidence of a *Queen*. Negative thoughts will come, but you do not have to let them stay and reside in your mind.

Vitamin D. Take in fresh air and soak in vitamin D, this is an important resource. Getting outside can be a great way to step away from stress. Getting out and help in being creative and problem-solving. Going for a peaceful walk can help the brain function in a way where you can think more clearly and get away from distractions. Going outside and being in sunlight can lift your mood and literally brighten your day. Always remember to have a balance of being both outside and inside.

Do not Overbook. It can become quite easy to take on many tasks and commit to numerous occasions. As a *Queen* you must know when to say *no* to some events or tasks. You cannot be everywhere or in two places at one time. Balance is key.

Take on a schedule that is doable for you and manageable, not overwhelming. Filling your day or week with too many tasks and obligations will run the risk of you falling behind on a task or having to cancel on an event. Think reasonably when it comes to your time.

Know You Are Loved. Always know that you are loved by God first, yourself second, and then by others. Knowing you are loved in this order will reassure you that you are always, and will be, loved. Knowing you are loved, and where that love comes from, will keep you from accepting treatment from others called love that you do not deserve. Loving yourself will help you to put yourself first, accept healthy love, and value the love you give to others.

Listen to Upbeat Music. A quick way to set up a positive and energetic atmosphere is to play upbeat and motivational music. Playing upbeat and positive music in the morning is a great way to start your day. Music can change one's mood, bring back positive memories, or be played to create new memories. Music encourages singing and dancing, to things that are essential to your mental health.

Gratitude. Setting aside time to think on the things you are grateful for and the people you appreciate is a good resource to stay grounded and humble.

Queen Resources and Reminders

Celebrate The Good

Call a Friend

Slow Down

Read the Bible

Trash Negative Thoughts

Vitamin D

Don't Overbook

Know You Are Loved

Listen to Upbeat Music

Pamper Yourself

Gratitude Log

Celebrate Gratitude

List six things you are grateful for:

1. _____

2. _____

3. _____

4. _____

5. _____

6. _____

Gratitude Log

People I'm Grateful For

List five people you are grateful for:

1._____

2._____

3._____

4._____

5._____

Gratitude Log

Challenge

Write one challenge and what
you are learning from it:

Challenge:

_____

_____

_____

_____

What I Am Learning:

_____

_____

_____

_____

Gratitude Log

Greatest Memories

List four of your fondest memories:

1._____

_____

2._____

_____

3._____

_____

4._____

_____

Queen Affirmations

I Was Not Made to Give Up.

***

Today I Will Learn and Grow.

***

I Am a Priority.

***

Today I Choose to Be Happy.

***

I Am Creating The Life of My Dreams.

***

I Can Make a Difference in This World.

I Am

A Queen

Because...

You Are a Queen

WALKING IT OUT AS A QUEEN

*R*eaching this point of the book, you can now say confidently that you are a *Queen*. Now all you must do is walk in that statement. Shower yourself in confidence. Remind yourself of your great qualities and strengths. Enter the room with a royal presence and navigate that room with grace. Always walk with your head held high. Be quick to give others a smile.

Remember that God laid your foundation, therefore, you should always stand on your beliefs, morals, and values. A *Queen* is who you are as a woman, beginning the day you were born. All one must do is pull her out.

Always keep in mind what sets a *Queen* apart from others. The *Queen* always perseveres in the face of difficulty. No matter the challenge, the *Queen* continues until she triumphs. A *Queen* trusts herself and her knowledge, therefore when she finds herself in difficult situations, she does not have a pity party and begins to give up. The *Queen* instantly begins to think about solutions rather than her problems. The *Queen* will empower herself by using her resources, tapping into the traits she has as a *Queen*, and believe she can overcome anything that is placed before her.

There is no doubt that with new changes comes challenges, however, with time, one can master anything. Now that you are a *Queen*, you must fully commit to this role and status for it to truly become who you are. Let being a Queen be permanent, not a temporary trend. Do not fear failure, see it as learning opportunities. Know that as a *Queen* you are living the best version of yourself. You have clarity and purpose and more than anything else each day you are blessed with, you can be a *Queen*. So, be a *Queen*.

Queen Status

Directions: Rate 0 to 5 how much you believe each statement. "0" means you do not believe it at all and "5" means you completely believe it. Take this quiz again at the completion of this book.

STATEMENT	RATING
19. I believe in myself.	_____
20. I know who I am.	_____
21. I am happy to be me.	_____
22. I like the way I look.	_____
23. I am just as valuable as others.	_____
24. I see my past as a learning experience, not a failure.	_____
25. I am a leader.	_____
26. I can handle criticism.	_____
27. I am proud of my accomplishments.	_____
28. I respect myself.	_____
29. I feel good when I receive compliments.	_____
30. I am not afraid of making mistakes.	_____
31. I would rather be me than someone else.	_____
32. I know my worth.	_____
33. I feel like a *Queen*.	_____
34. I love myself even when I am rejected by others.	_____
35. I ask for help when I need it.	_____
36. I do not worry about what others think of me.	_____

TOTAL SCORE: _____

0-30 points	Becoming a *Queen*.
31-60 points	A *Queen* in the Making
61-90 points	Walking as a *Queen*.

Made in the USA
Monee, IL
10 September 2021